Table of Contents

Note: This book is intended for advanced fighters. If you are a beginner looking for an effective program this one can be modified to suit you. Use the same program at lower intensities. If you have any physical problems (i.e. heart trouble) you will want to consult your physician first.

BOXING: Training

How you decided to train will determine how you do in the ring. Devoted preparation is the key to a successful fight. Training was never a burden to me. I loved to train. Training was a release from the everyday stresses.

I believe you are not really living if you are not working towards achieving a goal. That's why when I was training I felt good about myself and what I was doing with my time.

When training, train as though you are training for the heavy championship of the world. Give it your all. Remember that there is someone out there that you are going to have to fight. Ask yourself if you are giving all that you can give. Are you training harder than your opponent?

The person that works the hardest is going to win. I always wondered what my opponent was doing. How many miles does he run a day? How many rounds does he do on the punching bag? Is he sitting playing video games right now, or is he training?

If you are a fighter, a fight is unavoidable. Are you going to be prepared for that day? REMBER, THE PERSON THAT WORKS THE HARDEST AND THE SMARTEST IS GOING TO WIN THE FIGHT!

FINDING A GOOD GYM

Finding a good gym is important. You need a place where they have good equipment, good coaching and a variety of sparring partners. You may not want to go to a gym where there isn't enough equipment. You don't want to have to wait to get on a punching bag while you're in the middle of a workout.

Try getting into a place where they have some pro's training. You can pick up a lot from watching, listening, and talking to other fighters. Having a variety of sparring partners is important also. The more fighters mean the better chance you have to get a sparring partner that fights at your level.

For a while, the only sparring partners I had were professionals. The Light Heavy Weight Champion of the World at the time was one of my sparring partners. This didn't benefit me. I was just a beginner at the time. He basically used me as a punching bag.

After a fighter gets beat up sparring enough, they become defensive fighters. This means they spend more time defending themselves than going after their opponent and trying to get points. So when you find a gym, try setting yourself up with sparring partners that are more at your own level.

Prioritize Your Goals

Deciding what is important for you to achieve, and what is irrelevant is crucial to developing yourself mentally for the fight. You need only worry yourself with what matters in your fight. The less you place on your list of things to do, the more you can concentrate on those things you have on it (i.e. training, nutrition, etc.).

Everyday Goals

Build your self-confidence based on measured achievement of goals. Everyday set a particular goal and try to achieve it. Maybe you'll try to hit the bag 200 times in two minutes or go maybe go 5 rounds instead of 4.

The little things you set out to achieve and then actually do achieve will build your self-confidence. And self-confidence is one of the most important things a boxer can have.

How Goal Setting Helps Build Self-Confidence

Goal setting is probably the most effective way of building self-confidence. By setting measurable goals, achieving them, setting new goals, achieving them, and so on. You prove your ability to yourself.

You are able to prove to yourself that you are able to perform and achieve effectively. You can see and recognize and enjoy your achievement, and feel real self-worth in that achievement.

Importantly, by knowing what you are able to achieve, you are not setting yourself up for surprise failure - you almost always have a reasonably accurate assessment of what your abilities really are, which is unclouded by ego or vanity.

Keep a Journal of Goals

Writing down the goals you want to achieve and have achieved is a very useful habit to get into. For some reason, having them written down makes people want to achieve them even more.

Also having them written down reminds you of what you have achieved. Seeing the ones you have achieved makes going after the new goals easier because you've shown yourself that you can set and achieve goals.

Keep Your Goals Manageable

Don't set goals that are unrealistic. Don't make a goal of becoming world champion within your first year of boxing. Everything takes time and eventually comes.

Someone said once that it takes a person 1000 times to do something before they master it. Set goals that are not too hard, but not too easy. Work your way up the ladder slowly or you may fall off that ladder in a very disappointing way.

Judge Yourself on Effort

Set performance goals, not outcome goals. You should only feel like a loser if you didn't give it your all. You can only expect to do your best. Sometimes that means you're not going to win. And that's O.K.

MUSIC

Most people like to listen to music while training. Try to find some music that motivates you. Tastes will vary. I knew a guy who liked to listen to classical music while he trained. Of course we made him wear headphones. If you're working out in a gym, try to find something everyone likes. Some music may be distracting to others.

STRETCHING

Stretching should be done long enough until you at least break a sweat (about 5 – 10 minutes). You don't want to pull a muscle the day before a fight and throw weeks of training away. Stretch each muscle to around a 10 second count. Make sure to stretch the calve muscles. Most of your movements require your calves.

WARMING UP

Warming up should include the stretching and some shadow boxing. Shadow fighting should begin slowly with fluid motion. Don't start snapping punches right away. Let your muscles stretch a little first then increase speed gradually until you feel loose.

DIET

Maintain a diet that is high in carbohydrates and fluids. Take vitamins. Keep a high level of vitamin C in your system. This will keep you from getting sick. You can't train effectively when you're sick.

Try to keep at your natural body weight. If you drop down below your natural body weight your body begins to feed off itself. Your body naturally uses the fat in your body as an energy source. When all your fat is used up, your body begins to consume your muscle tissue.

You can actually make yourself weaker if you train too hard. That's why you must provide your body with the proper amount of nutrients.

PUSHING YOURSELF

I always considered the true training to begin when I was at the point of exhaustion. In most fights, there comes a point when both fighters are exhausted. This is the defining moment. The fighter who decides to put forth that extra step is probably going to win.

It's called having "heart." A champion throws that extra combination when most fighters wouldn't. A champion keeps his hands up and defends himself when most fighters wouldn't. A champion gives two punches for every one received.

A champion goes that extra step. And where do you condition yourself to do that? You start with that attitude from the beginning and you carry it till the end.

If you constantly push yourself and say you can do more, you will become an effective fighter. Attitude is the main ingredient towards making a champion. So remember, YOUR TRAINING BEGINS WHERE MOST FIGHTER'S END.

DON'T OVERWORK MUSCLES

You shouldn't overwork muscles for too many consecutive days. Typically you should work muscles no more than 2 days in a row and then give them a rest by working other muscles. For example, work on punch combinations for a couple days then work your legs on others.

GIVE YOURSELF SOME MUCH NEEDED REST

It's hard for a dedicated fighter to take it easy and rest for a day. I remember feeling guilty if I didn't work out every day. But your muscles need rest and recovery time. They can't build up and come back stronger if they never get the chance. When you work a muscle, you break it down. Then it heels and recovers stronger than when you worked it. That's the process and rest has to be included in that process. Otherwise you're working for nothing other than to weaken yourself.

WRAPPING YOUR HANDS

Wrapping your hands properly is important. You should not wrap your hands so the wrapping is too tight. It should just be snug. When you wrap your hands, spread your fingers out and extend them outwards.

Put the end loop around your thumb and cross over the bottom of the hand and wrap around your wrist twice. Cross over the back of your hand and go around pinky and then back around your palm. Repeat this for each finger.

Then wrap twice around your knuckles. Make sure your knuckles are not being too constricted. Check by making a fist. If it feels too tight, then start over. Rap the remaining wraps around your wrist and secure with tape. If your fingers are getting too bruised during training, you may want to use two pairs of wraps.

Another method I sometimes used was using Maxi Pads and taping them over my knuckles. Sounds weird, but they work well. If using Maxi Pads is too embarrassing, then try using a softer bag like a water filled bag.

FINDING TIME TO TRAIN

The ideal time to train is the same time your fight is going to be. For example, if you know your fight is going to be around 7:00 p.m., you may want to schedule your training to be around that time. This way your body is in tune to when it is going to be most active.

Just like how you fall asleep at the same time and wake at the same time, you are the most effective physically at a certain time also. But with most of our schedules, we find time to train when we can. Not necessarily when we prefer.

USING IMAGERY

Using imagery means visualizing your opponent and what you want to do to him/her. Visualize him throwing punches at you and visualize hitting him/her. Imagery should be used throughout your training.

When shadow boxing, hitting the bag, during roadwork, or just lying in bed, you can train your mind anywhere. Just sitting in the dentist office you can imagine yourself in the ring fighting.

Try to feel yourself moving and throwing punches. If you go throw it enough in your head, it will become second nature when you actually do it.

SPARRING

Sparring is important in your training. This is where you can make mistakes and correct them. You can't do that in competition. You can work on defense one day and then more offense the next. You can try out new combinations during sparring sessions. This is practice for the actual fight.

Also, when you are sparring, you should not use 100% power in every punch. You should only use 50% to 60% most of the time and load up on your punches when you know you have a sure shot.

Pay attention to your breathing also. Exhale when you throw a punch. This will help regulate your breathing. Relax in the ring, even when you're being hit. Conserve every ounce of energy you can.

Sparring is where you learn your weaknesses and strengths. If you're dropping your left, your coach can see it and help you correct that. Or your sparring partner will let you know by popping you one when you do it.

Sparring should not be a negative part of your training. Make sure you are sparring with someone at your level or at least someone that isn't going to knock you around and use you as a punching bag.

Like I said earlier, if you get beat up every day during sparring, you will become a defensive fighter and you will not want to fight in a competition situation. Some fighters just learn to survive in the ring and never learn how to win.

I would rather you fight someone below your level than someone who is just going to knock you around. It's better to be accustomed to winning rather than losing.

Use petroleum jelly on your face to avoid getting cut or swelled up. Find a comfortable mouthpiece that won't fall out during sparring. I suggest keeping two or three and keeping them in a clean container free of germs.

I prefer using the mouthpiece that only covers the top bridge of your mouth. The double ones seem like they would be hard to breathe from. You need to be able to take in as much air as you can to give your muscles the oxygen they need.

Don't share mouthpieces. First off, it's not going to fit properly. Secondly, it's a quick way to get sick or spread your germs.

PACING YOURSELF

Work on pacing yourself during training. Get in the habit of throwing 3 to 4 punch combinations and then stepping to either side. Try to take a couple deep breaths between combinations.

It would be great if a fighter could throw punches non-stop, but no one can. Your body needs a rest even if it is only a second or two. I suggest hitting the bag with a quick 3 – 4 punch combination and stepping left or right. Never backwards (moving backwards keeps you in front of your opponent and in their striking range).

If you try throwing non-stop punches, you will quickly burn out. You'll be much more effective if you pace yourself and not try killing your opponent in the first round. Sometimes it's best to take it easy in the first round anyway.

This allows you time to figure out your opponent. If you rush in, you may make a painful mistake that could lose the fight for you. The only time you should load up and go hard at your opponent is when you know for sure that you can do it without being caught.

When you have your opponent in trouble you can explode on him/her. But make sure you leave enough in case he/she retaliates.

THROWING COMBINATIONS

If you are a beginner fighter, train yourself to throw 3 punch combinations. For example, throw a jab to the side gut, which will force your opponent to drop an arm to guard himself, then a quick jab to the head to knock his head back and pop his chin up. Then quickly and powerfully throw a straight right to his chin.

Your first punch is bait to open up for a two-punch assault. Professionals use a four punch combination, but I think beginners should use the three.

FEET WORK

Feet-work is important in BOXING. This is something that needs to be practiced everyday in training. It's what keeps you balanced and allows spring in your punches. NEVER CROSS YOUR FEET!

Always lead with the foot closest to the direction you are heading. If you are moving left, lead with your left foot and slide the right foot over. If you're going backward, lead with your back foot and slide your front one back after.

If you cross your feet, you're going to get knocked off balance or down on your butt. Keep your knees flexible to absorb a hit and allow spring in your punches.

ROAD WORK

When we mean roadwork, it is just that - work. When jogging, throw punches, run backwards, shuffle side to side, and if you feel you need to strengthen, carry weights (ankle and wrist weights are ideal). Doing sprints is a good idea also.

I sprint two telephone poles and then jog two at a slower pace. End your roadwork with a cool down walk of a quarter mile. Always dress for the season. If you catch a cold during training you may have just lost your fight.

BUILDING STRENGTH BY WEIGHT TRAINING

To increase your strength you need to use what they call the pyramid system, find your MAX (how much you can lift one time) and then subtract that by 50 lbs. Start out with that number. (ex. My MAX is 200 so I start out lifting 150).

Lift this weight 8 times, then increase by ten pounds and lift that 6, then again increase by ten pounds and lift that 4 and so on. When you get to one you should be ten pounds below your MAX.

Once you get to where you can lift every set without help then increase your MAX by 5 pounds next time you lift. Results from this are very good. To tighten your muscles just go with a low weight but doing many reps as possible.

SELF-ASSESSMENT

It's important to take initiative and do for yourself many things you would expect from your coach. Part of what you can do for yourself is peer assessment. Get acquainted with your sparring partners. Don't be afraid to ask them questions about your performance.

Ask them what they feel you did right and what you did wrong. And return the favor by telling them what they did right and what they did wrong. Belonging to a gym means you have many resources at your disposal - some being other fighters and trainers.

You can also do some self-assessment by keeping a journal. In this journal you can write down everything you learn. You can write down what is working for you or what is not working for you.

I often used a video camera to help give me some self-assessment. This helped enormously. I was able to see what I was doing wrong and what I was doing right. You can see if maybe you're dropping your left when you throw a right.

Maybe you will notice that you are not keeping your elbows in. Maybe your stance is too wide or not wide enough. Things like this you can really see when you use a video recorder. And it's also just nice to have a record of yourself to see where you started and where you ended.

3 DAYS BEFORE A FIGHT

Slow things down. You won't make any significant gains in the last 3 three days. This is a time for resting and storing up energy. I do suggest doing some slow running to keep your muscles loose.

At the most I would do 1- 2 miles a day barely breaking a sweat. Don't train vigorously during these last 3 days. You will burn up your stored energy, tear down muscle tissue, possibly cause unwanted injuries, etc.

Get good sleep for these 3 days. Avoid stress, and relax.

Since you're not training, spend your free time preparing your gear for the fight, making hotel reservations, getting directions, buying foods and beverages, etc. Don't wait to pack things the night before. There will always be something you forget and will need to get.

Go over your check list and start packing 3 days ahead of time. You don't have to do it all on the first day, but I suggest getting started early, and do a little here and there until you're ready.

If you wait till the night before, you may find yourself staying up way later than expected and running to the store when you should be sleeping (whether it be late at night or early in the morning). I usually have 90% if not all of it ready by the day before. It makes things much less stressful.

Load up on carbs like spaghetti and other pasta. Not too much meat sauce though. The grease can cause digestion problems you don't want (in other words - the poops).

THE NIGHT BEFORE A FIGHT

Have everything prepared and ready to go. You want to be able to wake up, eat, and jump in your car and go.

Load up early in the day on carbs. I say early, so the heavy food you eat has time to work its way through and get out. You don't want to feel heavy and bloated the day of the fight. Your late night meal should be something light like fish, salad, or both.

No greasy foods like burger or heavy foods like steak. You'll spend your fight morning bloated and slow. You want to feel light and fast during the fight.

Lay out your gear, making sure you leave nothing left out.

Make sure you start hydrating that night. A good way to gauge if you're properly hydrated is to look at your urine. If it's too yellow, then you're not hydrated enough. It should be clear or slightly tinted yellow.

Don't drink anything with caffeine or eat anything with sugar. You may be nervous enough, adding those two elements can make it much harder to get that valuable sleep. Actually, studies have shown, that the most important day to get good rest is 2 days before.

The Morning of the Fight

Wake up early to give yourself time to eat and get ready to go. Plan to finish eating 2 1/2 hours before your fight. That way you give your body time to digest the food. Eat a light breakfast full of energy foods such as grains. My favorite prefight breakfast is *WHEATIES FUEL* with a banana. Everyone has their own preference. Just make sure it's nothing heavy, greasy, or full of sugar.

Hydrate, but don't over hydrate. There is such a thing as drinking too much. Many things can go wrong with over hydrating. First, you'll feel bloated, you may get cramps, and racing with a full bladder sucks.

Again, go with the rule, if your urine is bright yellow, then you need more fluids. Your urine should be clear or slightly tinted. If it's clear, you're good to go and no need to overfill the tank.

If you're a coffee drinker, I suggest drinking it prefight. Studies have shown that caffeine can boost an athlete's performance. However, I think you should have some relationship with caffeine before consuming a bunch for a fight. Otherwise, if you're not used to caffeine, your stomach may not be able to handle it and you may get some nasty cramps and an upset stomach.

Psychology of Boxing:
Creating the
Perfect Fighter

by William Scanlan

Psychology of Boxing: Creating the Perfect Fighter

DON'T GET PSYCHED OUT

Sometimes it's best to not look at your opponent while you're waiting around for your fight. Your opponent may appear to be stronger than you are. He/she may look meaner or tougher than you. If your opponent seems to you to be more confidant, then you're going to start wondering what he has that makes him so confident.

All these things can intimidate you and psyche you out, especially if you're a beginner boxer who is not sure of your abilities yet. That's why I think it is more beneficial to avoid your boxing competition and pay no attention to him/her until you step in the ring and get busy.

HOW YOU ACT BEFORE A FIGHT

Find something to keep yourself busy until your fight. Bring a book to read, bring an IPOD, talk to your teammates and coach, etc. Just conversing or listening to other boxers can get you psyched out. If you start to listen about how tough other fighters think they are or how much more experience they have, then that may affect you mentally. Hearing how good others are may make you feel less of yourself and result in you getting psyched out.

I suggest wearing a set of headphones and not listening or talking to others until your fight. Find a quiet place to hang out until then. Take that time to relax and use imagery to prepare your mind for the fight.

If you've been videotaping yourself boxing training, then watch the tape on your camcorder. Sometimes watching yourself train will help trigger you into the zone you need to get into.

LET YOUR BOXING COMPETITION WORRY ABOUT YOU. NOT THE OTHER WAY AROUND

By keeping to yourself, you can keep your boxing competition wondering about you. Let their imagination run by being ambiguous. If you goof around and run your mouth before a boxing competition, then your boxing competition's going to take you as a punk.

Act like you could care less who you have to fight and pay no attention to the boxing competition. Let them look and wonder about you instead of you paying attention to them.

Don't act cocky though. In my experience, those who act cocky or overly tough are usually not the guys to worry about. The guys to worry about are the ones who are laid back minding their own business.

FEED OFF THE CROWD

Don't listen to the crowd when they boo. Remember, you're the one in there fighting and they're the ones standing back watching. 95% of the crowd would never have the courage to get in the ring and do what you have to. Let those punks who boo get in the ring and try it.

Feed off the crowd when they cheer. When the crowd is behind you, you get a burst of adrenaline. Nothing feels better when you have the crowd off their feet cheering you on.

OVER CONFIDENCE CAN KILL

Good confidence is great. Over confidence can kill you. Being overconfident leads to under-boxing training and risky fighting. Some boxers get it in their head that they are the best and because of that they don't have to train as hard. Never slack during boxing training. Push yourself always to do better.

Never underestimate your boxing competition and take risky chances in the ring. The moment you start taking too many risks is the moment you get knocked out. It only takes one punch from any fighter, good or bad, to knock you on your butt. Strive for perfection always and keep humble about your skills.

PUSH YOURSELF

I always considered the true boxing training to begin when I was at the point of exhaustion. In most fights, there comes a point when both fighters are exhausted. This is the defining moment. The boxer who decides to put forth that extra step is probably going to win.

It's called having "heart." A champion throws that extra combination when most fighters wouldn't. A champion keeps his hands up and defends himself when most fighters wouldn't.

A champion gives two punches for every one received. A champion goes that extra step. And where do you condition yourself to do that? In boxing training. You start with that attitude from the beginning and you carry it till the end.

If you constantly push yourself and say you can do more, you will become an effective boxer. Attitude is the main ingredient towards making a champion. So remember, YOUR BOXING TRAINING BEGINS WHERE MOST BOXER'S END.

SPARRING SHOULD BE A POSITIVE EXPERIENCE

Sparring is important in your boxing training. This is where you can make mistakes and correct them. You can't do that in boxing competition. You can work on more defense one-day and then more offense the next.

You can try out new combinations during sparring sessions. This is practice for the actual fight. Sparring is where you learn your weaknesses and strengths. If you're dropping your left, your coach can see it and help you correct that.

Or your sparring partner will let you know by popping you one when you do it. Sparring should not be a negative part of your boxing training. Make sure you are sparring with someone at your level or at least someone that isn't going to knock you around and use you as a punching bag.

Like I said earlier, if you get beat up every day during sparring, you will become a defensive boxer and you will not want to fight in a boxing competition situation. Some fighters just learn to survive in the ring and never learn how to win.

I would rather you fight someone below your level than someone who is just going to knock you around. It's better to be accustomed to winning rather than losing.

PUT YOUR TIME IN

It's easy to get discouraged if you're not excelling as fast as others. You have to put the time in before you can learn the skills. Your skill level depends on the amount of time and dedication you put in.

I remember wanting to be as good as the pro's and getting disappointed when I couldn't beat them sparring. But skill comes with time and experience. That's why you must judge yourself at your own level and not someone else's.

FEEL PROUD

I've played all sports and I've found boxing to be, by far, the most demanding and rewarding sport of them all. Boxing demands sacrifice and dedication. Someone who is lazy and undisciplined is not going to make it as a boxer.

To win in boxing, you must be an outstanding athlete. 90% of boxing is up to you. Your coaches can't make you an athlete they can only polish you up. The foundation has to already be there for a coach to build off from.

BOXING IS A STRESS RELIEVER

Boxing is a good way to relieve stress. Imagine the bag being someone you can't stand. You can bang away at it and not them. That way you relieve stress and not go to jail for taking your frustrations out on them. It gives you time to yourself away from the everyday hassles you may encounter.

You feel more in control when you have a good workout. Boxing builds self-esteem and lowers self-doubt. Thus creating a feeling of being in control. With more power over the stressful things in your life.

PRIORITIZING YOUR GOALS

Deciding what is important for you to achieve, and what is irrelevant is crucial to developing yourself mentally for the fight. You need only worry yourself with what matters in your fight. The less you place on your list of things to do, the more you can concentrate on those things you have on it (i.e. boxing training, nutrition, etc.).

SETTING EVERYDAY GOALS

Build your self-confidence based on measured achievement of goals. Everyday set a particular goal and try to achieve it. Maybe you'll try to hit the bag 200 times in two minutes or go maybe go 5 rounds instead of 4.

The little things you set out to achieve and then actually do achieve will build your self-confidence. And self-confidence is one of the most important things a boxer can have.

GOAL SETTING BUILDS SELF-CONFIDENCE

Goal setting is probably the most effective way of building self-confidence. By setting measurable goals and achieving them. Also setting new goals and achieving them, and so on. You prove your ability to yourself.

You are able to prove to yourself that you are able to perform and achieve effectively. You can see and recognize and enjoy your achievement, and feel real self-worth in that achievement.

Importantly, by knowing what you are able to achieve, you are not setting yourself up for surprise failure - you almost always have a reasonably accurate assessment of what your abilities really are, which is unclouded by ego or vanity.

KEEP A JOURNAL OF ACHIEVABLE GOALS

Writing down the goals you want to achieve and have achieved is a very useful habit to get into. For some reason, having them written down makes people want to achieve them even more.

Also having them written down reminds you of what you have achieved. Seeing the ones you have achieved makes going after the new goals easier because you've shown yourself that you can set and achieve goals.

KEEP GOALS REALISTIC

Don't set goals that are unrealistic. Don't make a goal of becoming world champion within your first year of boxing. Everything takes time and eventually comes.

Someone said once that it takes a person 1000 times to do something before they master it. Set goals that are not too hard, but not too easy. Work your way up the ladder slowly or you may fall off that ladder in a very disappointing way.

SET BOXING PERFORMANCE GOALS

Set boxing performance goals, not outcome goals. You should only feel like a loser if you didn't give it your all. You can only expect to do your best. Sometimes that means you're not going to win. And that's O.K.

YOUR MOOD IS UNDER YOUR CONTROL

Bad moods damage your motivation to succeed in boxing training or boxing competition. They make you more prone to negative thinking, and cause distraction, often as you trigger bad moods in other people.

Your mood is completely under your control - bad moods are something you cannot afford. You can improve your mood in the following ways:

- Through positive thinking - say to yourself 'I feel good' or 'I am going to move/punch faster' or 'I can feel energy pouring into my limbs'. This really does help.

- By treating each element of a boxing performance individually - when you make a mistake, refocus and concentrate on the next separate element of the boxing performance. Treating a boxing performance in this way ensures that a bad move or a missed punch does not affect following moves or punches.

- By using imagery - imagine a beautiful scene or a time when you were performing very well and feeling good. Alternatively, imagine feeling good.

GET YOURSELF PSYCHED!

The following techniques can be used to psyche yourself up:

- Warm up faster and harder

- Use imagery - for example, imagine yourself in a boxing match.

- Use positive talk - 'I can feel energy and strength flowing into me'

- Focus on what you need to do in the ring

BE CONSISTANT WITH YOUR WARM-UP ROUTINE

Many boxers do this by developing routines that help them to focus their minds and block out distractions.

These may involve rituals that involve preparation, detailed dressing rules, or precisely executed warm-ups. Part of this practiced routine might involve specific things such as imagery, positive thinking, mood control and distraction and stress management.

All of this ensures that you enter a competitive situation in a fighting state of mind to give an excellent boxing performance. Experiment with developing a ritual that covers all points of preparation that you consider being important. By practicing this ritual and keeping it standard in boxing training, it will be automatic and complete when you face a potentially stressful boxing competition.

Boxing Excellence

The following pointers should lead you to maximize your boxing abilities:

- Boxing training Excellence

- Set specific achievement goals before each boxing training session

- Prepare your mind before boxing training to get the most out of each period

- In boxing training, practice your skills with the maximum attention and effort

- Use imagery and simulation to mimic actual boxing performance as far as possible

- Boxing performance Excellence

- Rest effectively before a fight or boxing training day

Boxing
Punches and
Movement

by William Scanlan

Boxing Punches and Movement

Note: When I wrote this, I wrote it for the RIGHT HANDED person. If you are left hander, then modify it for a left hander.

Shadow Boxing

Shadow boxing consists of combining punch combinations, feet work, visualization of opponent, and breathing. I like to use shadow boxing to warm up. Start out with very slow movement and then progress into movement that is quick, under control, and carried out with great concentration. Always keep on the balls of your feet.

Shadow boxing is an excellent time to visualize your opponent and what you want to do to him. Try to visualize your opponent throwing a punch and then create a combination to counter that punch. Then at your own pace practice that combination.

Defensive stance

I consider there to be two defensive stances – a straight up defensive stance and a leaning back defensive stance. The straight up stance is where you have your feet a little more than shoulder width apart, and your weight is balanced on both feet. Stand on the balls of your feet. This gives you balance and spring in both your steps and your punches.

Your knees need to be bent slightly so you can spring into action quickly. Put your gloves up around your chin to protect it and hold your elbows in close to your sides to protect your ribs and kidney area. Tuck your chin down to protect it. Your shoulders should be raised a little to protect your chin also. Your left shoulder should be slightly more forward than your right (if that is your jabbing arm).

This way you're not as big a target for your opponent and your jab is out in front to steer your opponent. Also with your right back a little it is ready in a cocked position ready to fly

Remember to keep loose. All your muscles need to be loose including your hands. Relax as much as possible. Fighting is stressful and causes your body to tense up. Veteran fighters learn to be relaxed in the ring even when they are being hit. Tensing up uses valuable energy. You need to conserve every ounce of energy you can. I had a trainer that wouldn't let me stand up out of my corner chair during a fight. He would actually pick me up out of the chair and on to my feet just to conserve that little amount of energy.

The second defensive stance is what I call the leaning back stance. It basically includes everything the above does but the difference is your weight rests on your back foot instead of balanced on both feet. So you're actually leaning back. This method could be dangerous though because of the weight distribution being placed on your back foot. It's easier to be knocked off balance in this position.

But I liked this position because it gave the illusion that I was at a farther striking distance from my opponent than I actually was. Your opponent feels safer, so is less defensive. At the right moment you can quickly spring forward and be within your striking distance and unleash your combination of punches. It gives you the element of surprise. Also, I liked it because by springing forward like that it gave my punches more momentum

Keep Your Chin Tucked Down

Always keep your chin tucked down into your chest. A veteran fighter will always aim for your chin. This is the most common way people get knocked out. The chin is filled with nerves and when you are hit solid on it the billions of nerves in it overload and cause you to black out.

Also keep your shoulders up a little to protect the chin further. When your opponent throws a punch you can deflect that punch using your shoulder. Their punch will bounce of your shoulder and away from your chin

During training you need to get in the habit of keeping your chin down. Some of the "old timers" would take a tennis ball and tuck it under their chin while they shadow boxed. If you work out with a friend or are lucky enough to have a trainer, have them watch to make sure you are keeping your chin tucked.

Hit and Move

When you hit your opponent, move to one side or the other. Never back up. When you back up you're keeping yourself in front of your opponent and within his striking range. You're also on the move, so you're not balanced as much as if you were stationary. If you move to one side then your opponent has to realign himself to effectively throw a punch. If they try to throw a punch when you're off to the side, they will not have nearly the amount of power or effectiveness as if you were in front of them.

When you're moving to the side, leave your opponent with a punch. If you're moving to the left, hit him with your right. If you're moving to the right, hit him with your left. You're creating momentum by moving one way or the other and you should use that momentum and apply it to a good solid punch.

Don't just stand there either after hitting your opponent. This is one of the biggest mistakes beginner boxers make. You've just unleashed a flurry of punches on your opponent. Your body is tired. Your opponent covered up and took a breather while you were hitting him. He's now refreshed and ready to hit you. Don't just stand there and let him do it. Move away.

Let him come to you. Get away and give yourself an extra second to catch a breath and get into your defensive stance. Boxing is normally one fighter throwing a combination and then the other fighter throwing a combination and it goes back and forth like that. The great fighters are masters at throwing counter punches and frustrating their opponents.

Feet Work

Boxing is a matter of movements. How well you move your feet determines how well you box. Fast feet lead to fast punches. If you are slow on your feet, then you're slow with your fists. You use your feet to seek your opponent and to avoid your opponent. Feet work must be graceful and fluid. It should be done easy and relaxed but firm in movement. Proper feet work leads to harder hitting power and speed. Quick feet work will beat any punch. A moving target is harder to hit.

The best position for your feet is where you can quickly move in any direction and cover a distance quickly. Your feet should be a little more than shoulder width apart. To move, slide your feet or shuffle. NEVER CROSS YOUR FEET! If your opponent hits you with your feet crossed, you will lose your balance, stumble or go down.

Always lead with the foot closest to the direction you are heading. If you are moving left, lead with your left foot and slide the right foot over. If you're going backward, lead with your back foot and slide your front one back after. If you cross your feet, you're going to get knocked down.

Keep on the balls of your feet. This helps with agility, absorption, and spring in your punches. Keep your knees bent slightly. This will give you spring in your punches and help absorb a punch. Never stand squared up to your opponent with your weight on your heals. Your grandma could knock you over if you were standing that way.

Breathing

Breathing is important in boxing. Learning to control your breathing during a fight is crucial. Many beginner boxers hold their breath during a fight. They get nervous and forget to breathe. This affects the body in many ways. Muscles need oxygen to function. The less air you give your muscles the harder they have to work. Thus the less you breathe the quicker you get tired.

Also, it is extremely painful to get hit in the gut or in the ribs while holding your breath. The only time I went down on the canvas is when I got caught holding my breath and someone nailed me in the ribs. I would rather get knocked out by being hit in the head than being put on the canvas that way. When someone hits you in the gut or ribcage, exhale and let that pressure in your lungs escape.

A way to control your breathing is by getting into the habit of exhaling when you throw a punch. Sometimes when you watch boxing and you hear that hissing noise when a boxer throws a punch – that's not air escaping from his gloves. That's him exhaling when he throws a punch. This method can also intimidate your opponent. The sound of the hissing reminds him that he is being hit and you have control of the fight for that moment.

Keep Arms and Hands loose

It's hard not to tighten up during a fight. The adrenaline released on your body causes your muscles to tighten. When you tighten your body up you expend valuable energy. Try tightening every muscle in your body for two minutes and see how much energy you lose. Many beginner boxers stay tight like that for a whole fight and find themselves exhausted.

You need to train yourself to stay loose. Even when you're being hit. When you throw a punch, all muscles should be loose right up till the moment of impact.

Snap Your Punches

Most people think that the more muscle in an arm the harder that person can hit. That's not necessarily true. IT'S THE SNAP IN THE PUNCH THAT CAUSES THE MOST DAMAGE. Your arms need to be like wet towels and you need to snap them out.

The power of a punch is at the end of a punch. This means that when your fist strikes your opponent your arm is fully extended. By doing this, you have more leverage on your punches and thus you have more power. Also, when you throw a punch you build up momentum and energy.

Then right when your arm is fully extended the momentum and energy that has been built up releases and explodes into a very effective punch.

Bruce Lee had a punch he called the "One inch punch." He would stick his hand one inch away from a volunteer and with the energy he created from a quick twist of his hip he could transferred that energy through his body to his fist and knock that volunteer of his feet.

Head Movement

Head movement is very important to get in the habit of doing. Boxers are very effective when they come at an opponent moving their head from side to side. It's much harder to hit a moving target. Make sure when you're moving your head it doesn't throw off your balance.

The movement should come from bending your knees and bending at the waist, always keeping your balance. This is best for shorter boxers working their way in on taller boxers. Also, make sure you don't move into a punch. By moving into a punch you will increase the power of your opponent's punch.

Hit With Knuckles Not Fingers

Hit the bag with your top knuckles and not your finger knuckles. This will give you a solid punch and reduce chances of injury. A lot of boxers make the mistake of slapping their punches. This means they hit with the knuckles of their fingers. When they do this, their punches are not solid ones, their fingers act as shock absorbers.

It's hard to notice if you're doing this with big puffy boxing gloves on. You need to concentrate on your punches and feel for the impact on your knuckles. Look for those solid punches. Sometimes it is beneficial to train with the thin leather bag gloves. They allow you to fully feel how you're hitting. You'll know if you're hitting with your finger knuckles and not your top knuckles.

Circling Your Opponent

If you know what handed your opponent is, being left or right handed, you need to circle your opponent in the direction away from their power hand. For example, if your opponent is right handed, circle to his left because his right hand will be his power hand. This will keep you out of his power range and keep you from getting knocked out.

It's the same concept as hitting and moving. You don't want to be in front of your opponent where he can inflict the most damage to you. It also goes along with head movement. A moving target is harder to hit. Sugar Ray Leonard beat Marvin Hagler this way. He was always a step ahead of Marvin and never allowed Marvin to post up on him.

When you circle your opponent, keep on the balls up your feet. Never rest on your heels, because if you receive a solid blow you will be knocked backwards or even down. Keeping on the balls of your feet will help you maintain your balance. And remember to not cross your feet.

Use Your Free Arm To Protect Your Body

A common mistake all boxers make when they throw a punch is dropping their free hand. When you throw a punch, use the other hand to protect yourself. If you throw a right, keep your left up to protect your head.

Make sure when you throw a punch that you snap the hand you punched with directly back to your face. This will protect you against any counter punches your opponent may throw.

Control Your Punches – Don't overthrow

Make sure your punches are kept in close and not flaying around. Haymakers are not effective punches. Keep your punches under control. If you throw an out of control punch and miss, your opponent is going to make you pay for it.

First thing that will happen is your body is going to have to expend extra energy to compensate for your miss because you overshot your target and all your momentum is pulling you forward. This will cause you to be unbalanced.

Next your opponent is going to realize your mistake and take advantage of you while you are regaining your balance. He'll hit you and probably cause you to be even more unbalanced, which means even more energy loss for you. And mentally you're going to be mad because you missed and gave your opponent that advantage over you.

Dig With Your Knuckles

What this means is that when you make contact with your opponent you dig your knuckles into whatever area you're hitting. It's just a simple flick of the wrist with your knuckles grinding into your opponent. Actually try to dig or scrape whatever part of the body you're targeting.

This will increase the power of your punch a lot. It also keeps a boxer from hitting with his fingers and absorbing the punch into his fingers. You can feel the solidness of this punch and so can your opponent.

Slip

Practicing slips is just as much mental as it is physical. A slip is basically ducking a punch. To slip a punch, you twist at the hips, bend at the knees, and bend slightly forward always keeping your eyes on your opponent. When practicing this maneuver you must visualize your opponent throwing a punch. Remember to stay on the balls of your feet.

If possible, throw out a jab or a hook to the body the same time you slip your opponents punch. Whenever a punch is thrown there is always an opening to hit on the person throwing the punch. A jab usually means the rib cage under the jabbing arm is open.

An uppercut usually leaves your opponent open for a hook to the head. A right hand is hard to counter because the left side of the head is protected from the left hand and the right shoulder protects the right side to the head. The way to counter a straight right is by an overhand right, an uppercut or a hook to the rib cage.

Outside Punches

What I mean by outside punches is punches that you should throw when your opponent is at the end of your punch and not coming in at you and in your chest. Outside punches use the most energy because you're reaching out to your opponent.

Once your opponent is farther away, he will have a greater reaction time to react to your punch. So an outside punch cannot be a lazy punch. It must be quick and delivered with damaging intentions. Outside punches include the jab, overhand right and straight right.

The Jab

The jab is done by holding your hand up high with your elbow in close to your body. Push off your back foot like a pitcher. Step forward with your forward foot and snap your arm straight out at your target. Rotate your fist over (thumb turns inward) as you reach full extension.

Keep your chin tucked into your shoulder to protect your head. You don't need to use a lot of power in this punch. It's used to bait, steer, frustrate, blind, and knock your opponent off balance. It doesn't have to be a powerful punch but it does have to be quick. If done quickly and carefully, the jab is probably your safest punch.

The jab is perfect for baiting your opponent. For example, throw a jab to the body and when your opponent goes to protect his midsection, come up quick with a straight right and a hook to the head. Or throw a jab to the head. Your opponent will keep his guard up to his head and you can quickly drop down and bang away at his body.

You use the jab to steer your opponent by knocking him to one side or the other. You can also steer him by using your jab as bait. Throw out the jab with intentions of moving quickly to one side or the other. Your opponent will counter your jab and follow you in the direction you are moving.

You can frustrate your opponent by continuously sticking him with your jab. Just pepper away at him if you know you're quicker than he is. Every time he throws a punch beat him with a quick jab. It drives a boxer crazy when their opponent constantly has their glove in his face.

When you keep your glove in your opponent's face, you blind him. It's hard to see with a glove constantly in face. A boxer's sight is limited already with their own gloves in their face. By adding your glove to the picture you make it even worse.

Using the jab correctly with enough power can unbalance your opponent. An unbalanced fighter is a vulnerable fighter. Knock your opponent from one side to the other or backward. When you see that your opponent is unbalanced, unleash your combinations and make him pay.

Straight Right

Straight rights are your power punches. These push people back and knock them out. To do a straight right, swing your right hip toward your opponent and release your shoulder as you snap your right arm out, make sure your palm is down. Your right heel should swing out also.

If your heel is swinging outward than that means you're getting proper rotation in your body. Extend your punch, but don't lock your elbow. Tuck your chin down into your right shoulder to protect your chin. Keep your left glove up to protect the left side of your chin. Dig with your knuckles. Actually try to scrape their nose or chin off with your knuckles.

Then snap your right hand back to your face to protect your face and move your hips to their original stance.

Overhand Right

The overhand right is an effective counter punch. When your opponent throws out a lazy jab or straight right, you should counter punch with an overhand right. An overhand right is done basically like the straight right but your punch goes over their punch.

Another difference is that it is comparable to throwing a baseball. You have more swing in your punch. You really need to keep your guard up when throwing this punch. If they are throwing a punch, you need to deflect or slip that punch. You can deflect it by either deflecting his punch with your left or deflect it with your shoulder.

Inside Punches

Inside punches are punches you throw when your opponent is in close to you or coming in on you. These punches don't require as much energy but are more difficult to throw because they are more awkward than your outside punches. Also, these punches don't allow as much reaction time for your opponent.

Left Hook

The left hook is a power punch thrown to the body or head. It is more difficult to throw than a straight punch, but it is also more difficult for your opponent to defend against because it comes from the side and allows less time for reaction. This punch lands with your elbow in a perpendicular position and your arm parallel to the floor, palm facing your body.

Start from your basic stance and turn your hips to the left. Keep your shoulders aligned with your hips. Keep your back foot planted as an anchor. Pivot on the ball of your front foot, turning your hips to the right as you roll your shoulder and release your punch.

Your hips move with this punch to give you power. Keep your elbow bent at 90 degrees until contact with your opponent, and then use your momentum to recoil to the ready position. Remember to keep your right glove up to protect your chin and tuck your chin down into your left shoulder but keep your eyes on your opponent.

Right Hook

The right hook to the body is similar to the left hook. Power still comes from your hip, but this time your front foot is used for stability. With this punch you can't reach out as far as with the left hook.

Your striking area is limited because it is coming from the right side of your body. This punch lands with your elbow in a perpendicular position and your arm parallel to the floor, palm facing your body.

Start from your basic stance, bend your knees (remember, this punch goes to the body), and turn your hips to the right. Keep your shoulders aligned with your hips. Keep your front foot planted as an anchor. Pivot on the ball of your back foot, turning your hips to the left as you roll your shoulder and release your punch.

Your hips move with this punch to give you power. Keep your elbow bent at 90 degrees until contact with your opponent then use your momentum to recoil to the ready position.

Remember to keep your left glove up by your chin to protect it. Tuck your chin down into your right shoulder but keep your eyes on your opponent.

Uppercut

An uppercut is a punch with a short upward arc that lands with your palm facing your body and your fist pointed toward the ceiling. You can throw either a left or right uppercut to the body or head. The power comes from your lower body and the upward thrust of your hips.

Bend your knees and tuck the elbow of the punching arm into your hip. From this deep bend, thrust upward with your hips and drive your punch upward. Keep your elbow bent at a 90-degree angle or more.

Aim for your opponent's chest and bounce your punch off his chest. This will help make sure you get up and under the chin to drive it upward. An excellent punch to follow up instantly after the uppercut is a sharp snapping hook to the head.

Boxing:
What to
Do in the
Ring

by William Scanlan

What to do in the Ring

First Things First

Make sure you put in your best fitting mouth piece. You don't want to have to be in the middle of a fight and have your mouth piece fall out. Also, make sure there are no chemicals in your hair or on your face.

Once you start sweating these chemicals such as hair spray may drip down into your eyes and irritate them. This could alter your vision or distract you from what you need to do your opponent.

Make sure your face is properly lubricated so you can avoid getting cut. Getting cut will not only take you out of the fight, but also prohibit you from competing in a fight you may have the next week or following week. If you're fighting amateur, make sure your head gear is one that fits well.

Often when you fight on and amateur team you have to share equipment, make sure ahead of time that you have the proper gear ready for you when your fight comes up.

Show Good Sportsmanship

Always show good sportsmanship. You are reflection of your team and your coach. People root for the boxer they like the most. Most spectators don't like cocky boxers.

Most amateur boxing tournaments are invite only. If boxers on your team are rude and unsportsmanlike, you probably won't be invited to many tournaments. This could even influence the judges in your fight.

I suggest before a fight tapping gloves with the other fighter. Don't complain if you get a bad call. And at the end of the fight, go shake hands with the other team.

Set Your Defensive stance

I consider there to be two defensive stances – a straight up defensive stance and a leaning back defensive stance. The forward stance is where you have your feet a little more than shoulder width apart, and your weight is balanced on both feet. Stand on the balls of your feet. This gives you balance and spring in both your steps and your punches.

Your knees need to be bent slightly so you can spring into action quickly. Put your gloves up around your chin to protect it and hold your elbows in close to your sides to protect your ribs and kidney area. Tuck your chin down to protect it. Your shoulders should be raised a little to protect your chin also.

Your left shoulder should be slightly more forward than your right (if that is your jabbing arm). This way you're not as big a target for your opponent and your jab is out in front to steer your opponent. Also with your right back a little it is ready in a cocked position ready to fly.

The second defensive stance is what I call the leaning back stance. It basically includes everything the above does but the difference is your weight rests on your back foot instead of balanced on both feet. So you're actually leaning back. This method could be dangerous though because of the weight distribution being placed on your back foot.

It's easier to be knocked off balance in this position. But I liked this position because it gave the illusion that I was at a farther striking distance from my opponent than I actually was.

Your opponent feels safer, so is less defensive. At the right moment you can quickly spring forward and be within your striking distance and unleash your combination of punches. It gives you the element of surprise. Also, I liked it because by springing forward like that it gave my punches more momentum.

Remember to keep loose. All your muscles need to be loose including your hands. Relax as much as possible. Fighting is stressful and causes your body to tense up. Veteran fighters learn to be relaxed in the ring even when they are being hit. Tensing up uses valuable energy.

You need to conserve every ounce of energy you can. I had a trainer that wouldn't let me stand up out of my corner chair during a fight. He would actually pick me up out of the chair and on to my feet just to conserve that little amount of energy.

Keep Your Chin Tucked Down

Always keep your chin tucked down into your chest. A veteran fighter will always aim for your chin. This is the most common way people get knocked out. The chin is filled with nerves and when you are hit solid on it the billions of nerves in it overload and cause you to black out.

Also keep your shoulders up a little to protect the chin further. When your opponent throws a punch you can deflect that punch using your shoulder. Their punch will bounce of your shoulder and away from your chin.

During training you need to get in the habit of keeping your chin down. Some of the "old timers" would take a tennis ball and tuck it under their chin while they shadow boxed.

If you work out with a friend or are lucky enough to have a trainer, have them watch to make sure you are keeping your chin tucked. So as you can guess, when you take an offensive position you should aim for the chin when throwing a punch. The best time catch your opponent is when they step into your punch.

This gives you not only the momentum of your arm hitting them, but also the momentum of your opponent running into you.

Hit and Move

When you hit your opponent, move to one side or the other. Never back up. When you back up you're keeping yourself in front of your opponent and within his striking range. You're also on the move, so you're not balanced as much as if you were stationary.

If you move to one side then your opponent has to realign himself to effectively throw a punch. If they try to throw a punch when you're off to the side, they will not have nearly the amount of power or effectiveness as if you were in front of them.

When you're moving to the side, leave your opponent with a punch. If you're moving to the left, hit him with your right. If you're moving to the right, hit him with your left. You're creating momentum by moving one way or the other and you should use that momentum by applying it to a good solid punch.

Don't just stand there either after hitting your opponent. This is one of the biggest mistakes beginner boxers make. You've just unleashed a flurry of punches on your opponent. Your body is tired. Your opponent covered up and took a breather while you were hitting him. He's now refreshed and ready to hit you. Don't just stand there and let him do it. Move away. Let him come to you. Get away and give yourself an extra second to catch a breath and get into your defensive stance.

Boxing is normally one fighter throwing a combination and then the other fighter throwing a combination and it goes back and forth like that. The great fighters are masters at throwing counter punches and frustrating their opponents.

Hit at an Angle

If possible, avoid squaring up against your opponent. If you square up against him, you place yourself in his power range. Try throwing your punches off to the side at an angle. This way your opponent has to reach around to you because you are not directly in front of him/her.

Some call it the triangle method. Pretend there is a triangle between yourself and your opponent. The tip of the angle should be pointing towards your opponent. When you throw your punch, you should be at one of the base vertexes of the imaginary triangle. Using this imagery can help you avoid squaring up with your opponent.

Tying up Your Opponent

When your opponent is getting the best of you, it is best to tie him up and hold on until the referee splits you apart. Sometimes you're just too tired to try and get away.

Tying up consists of getting in close to your opponent and holding his arms between your body and your arms. When you have him/her held in this position you can turn him one way or another or just hold on until you gather your breath.

It's also an effective way to get yourself out of a corner or off the ropes. Make sure you do not do it too many times or you may lose a point by deduction. Also, make sure you tuck your head into his shoulder.

Cutting off the Ring

Sometimes your opponent will run from you. Either he/she is hurt, scared, or trying to get in at you from an angle. To stop this, you must cut off the ring. Cutting off the ring means to trap your opponent in a corner or against the ropes.

To do this you must gradually push him to spot you want him by stepping in front of the direction he is going. Think of it as trying to catch a chicken in a chicken pen. The chicken tries running one way so you step in front of it.

Then it turns to go the other way so you step in front of it again but step forward a little more. You do this until it has nowhere to go. The same concept goes when trying to cut the ring off from your opponent.

This is important to do especially when your opponent is beating you to the punch and hitting you from an angle. You'll have to get the person trapped and in front of you so you can take control of the fight.

While Resting between Rounds

You have a minute rest between rounds. Take this time to relax and gather information and instruction from your corner. Take deep breaths up until the bell rings. Your muscles need as much oxygen you can give them.

Some people say it's better to breathe in through your nose and out through your mouth. I disagree, the only reason you should breathe through your nose is because your nose filters the air going into your mouth. Over the long run, this is a good idea. But in a fight you need as much oxygen as you can get.

If you've been boxing for awhile you probably have crushed nasal passages anyway and can't breathe so well through them. So I suggest breathing through the biggest air entrance you have and that's your mouth. Get as much air as you can and feed the muscles the air they are lacking.

Listen to your corner men. They see what you cannot. They see what's working for you and what is not. They can see when your opponent is dropping his guard or stepping off balance. Gather as much information from them as you can and use it.

Don't drink too much water. You should drink plenty of fluids before your fight. If you drink during the fight, you will cramp up and slow down. Too much water can lose the fight for you.

Hide Your Weakness

I always knew when I had a fight won. The moment I knew my opponent was hurt I took total control of the fight and punished my opponent for letting me know he was hurt. And that's how all boxers work. They keep pecking away until they find a weakness and then they exploit that weakness.

If you get hurt, it's best to try and hide it until the bell rings and you have time to recover. Don't give your opponent the advantage by showing him/her that he/she hurt you. They will gain confidence and punish you.

Don't Act Tired After a Fight

Sometimes how you act after a fight can sway a judge one way or another. Do not act tired after a fight when the judges are making their final decisions. This means, do not lay hunched over the ropes.

Don't sit down on a stool or especially the mat. Walk around with your hands on your hips or up on top of your head to get a better breath. Try and show that you had control of that fight and you deserve the win.

Never Come at Your Opponent Head First

Make sure you are in your defensive stance with your hands up and you're standing straight up. Never put your head out in front of you. It makes for an easy target if it's sticking out in front of you. You are open for an uppercut when you do that.

Keep your back vertical and your chin down and tucked away. And always make sure your hands are up around your chin with your elbows held in close to your body. NEVER BEND DOWN!

Strike First

If you can strike first and keep control of the fight then do it. This means you have to be quick and ready to throw an array of combinations. Hit, move, and then recoup.

Hit, move, and then recoup. Keep doing this as long as you don't burn yourself up in the first round. Watch for counter-punches. Keep your free arm up and protecting your chin.

Counter Punching

Counter punching is one of the most effective techniques for winning a fight. To counter punch, you must anticipate your opponents punch and decide on a punch to give in return to the one he/she is giving you. Hopefully you can connect with yours before your opponent connects with his/hers.

Counter punches frustrate your opponents to no end. If you connect with a punch every time they throw theirs, then you are telling them that they are too slow and you already have them figured out. You'll force your opponent to mix things up and throw combinations that they are not so comfortable throwing.

An example of a counter punch would be to throw an overhand right when your opponent throws out a lazy jab. Knock their jab to the side by brushing your overhand right in the inside of their jab. So the result is, their jab deflects off your overhand right and your overhand right gets through and hopefully connects to their jaw.

Feet Work

Boxing is a matter of movements. How well you move your feet determines how well you box. Fast feet lead to fast punches. If you are slow on your feet, then you're slow with your fists. You use your feet to seek your opponent and to avoid your opponent. Feet work must be graceful and fluid.

It should be done easy and relaxed but firm in movement. Proper feet work leads to harder hitting power and speed. Quick feet work will beat any punch. A moving target is harder to hit.

The best position for your feet is where you can quickly move in any direction and cover a distance quickly. Your feet should be a little more than shoulder width apart. To move, slide your feet or shuffle. NEVER CROSS YOUR FEET! If your opponent hits you with your feet crossed, you will lose your balance, stumble or go down.

Always lead with the foot closest to the direction you are heading. If you are moving left, lead with your left foot and slide the right foot over. If you're going backward, lead with your back foot and slide your front one back after. If you cross your feet, you're going to get knocked down.

Keep on the balls of your feet. This helps with agility, absorption, and spring in your punches. Keep your knees bent slightly. This will give you spring in your punches and help absorb a punch. Never stand squared up to your opponent with

41

your weight on your heals. Your grandma could knock you over if you were standing that way.

Breathing

Breathing is important in boxing. Learning to control your breathing during a fight is crucial. Many beginner boxers hold their breath during a fight. They get nervous and forget to breathe.

This affects the body in many ways. Muscles need oxygen to function. The less air you give your muscles the harder they have to work. Thus the less you breathe the quicker you get tired.

Also, it is extremely painful to get hit in the gut or in the ribs while holding your breath. The only time I went down on the canvas is when I got caught holding my breath and someone nailed me in the ribs.

I would rather get knocked out by being hit in the head than being put on the canvas that way. When someone hits you in the gut or ribcage, exhale and let that pressure in your lungs escape.

A way to control your breathing is by getting into the habit of exhaling when you throw a punch. Sometimes when you watch boxing and you hear that hissing noise when a boxer throws a punch – that's not air escaping from his gloves. That's him exhaling when he throws a punch.

This method can also intimidate your opponent. The sound of the hissing reminds him that he is being hit and you have control of the fight for that moment.

Keep Arms and Hands Loose

It's hard not to tighten up during a fight. The adrenaline released on your body causes your muscles to tighten. When you tighten your body up you expend valuable energy.

Try tightening every muscle in your body for two minutes and see how much energy you lose. Many beginner boxers stay tight like that for a whole fight and find them exhausted.

You need to train yourself to stay loose even when you're being hit. When you throw a punch, all muscles should be loose up till the moment of impact.

Snap Your Punches

Most people think that the more muscle in an arm the harder that person can hit. That's not necessarily true. IT'S THE SNAP IN THE PUNCH THAT CAUSES THE MOST DAMAGE. Your arms need to be like wet towels and you need to snap them out.

The power of a punch is at the end of a punch. This means that when your fist strikes your opponent your arm is full extended. By doing this, you have more leverage on your punches and thus you have more power. Also, when you throw a punch you build up momentum and energy.

Then right when your arm is fully extended the momentum and energy that has been built up releases and explodes into a very effective punch.

Bruce Lee had a punch he called the "One inch punch." He would stick his hand one inch away from a person and with the energy he created from a quick twist of his hip he could transferred that energy through his body to his fist and knock that person of his feet.

Head Movement

Head movement is very important to get in the habit of doing. Boxers are very effective when they come at an opponent moving their head from side to side. It's much harder to hit a moving target. Make sure when you're moving your head it doesn't throw off your balance.

The movement should come from bending your knees and bending at the waist, always keeping your balance. This is best for shorter boxers working their way in on taller boxers. Also, make sure you don't move into a punch. By moving into a punch you will increase the power of your opponent's punch.

Hit With Knuckles Not Fingers

Hit the bag with your top knuckles and not your finger knuckles. This will give you a solid punch and reduce chances of injury. A lot of boxers make the mistake of slapping their punches.

This means they hit with the knuckles of their fingers. When they do this, their punches are not solid ones, their fingers act as shock absorbers. It's hard to notice if you're doing this with big puffy boxing gloves on. You need to concentrate on your punches and feel for the impact on your knuckles.

Look for those solid punches. Sometimes it is beneficial to train with the thin leather bag gloves. They allow you to fully feel how you're hitting. You'll know if you're hitting with your top knuckles and not your top finger knuckles.

Circling Your Opponent

If you know what handed your opponent is, being left or right handed, you need to circle your opponent in the direction away from their power hand. For example, if your opponent is right handed, circle to his left because his right hand will be his power hand.

This will keep you out of his power range and keep you from getting knocked out. It's the same concept has hitting and moving. You don't want to be in front of your opponent where he can inflict the most damage to you.

It also goes along with head movement. A moving target is harder to hit. Sugar Ray Leonard beat Marvin Hagler this way. He was always a step ahead of Marvin and never allowed Marvin to post up on him.

When you circle your opponent, keep on the balls up your feet. Never rest on your heels, because if you receive a solid blow you will be knocked backwards or even down. Keeping on the balls of your feet will help you maintain your balance. And remember to not cross your feet.

Use Your Free Arm to Protect Your Body

A common mistake all boxers make when they throw a punch is dropping their free hand. When you throw a punch, use the other hand to protect yourself. If you throw a right, keep your left up to protect your head.

Make sure when you throw a punch that you snap the hand you punched with directly back to your face. This will protect you against any counter punches your opponent may throw.

Control Your Punches – Don't overthrow

Make sure your punches are kept in close and not flaying around. Hay-makers are not effective punches. Keep your punches under control. If you throw an out-of-control punch and miss, your opponent is going to make you pay for it.

First thing that will happen is your body is going to have to expend extra energy to compensate for your miss because you overshot your target and all your momentum is pulling you forward. This will cause you to be unbalanced. Next your opponent is going to realize your mistake and take advantage of you while you regain your balance.

He'll hit you and probably cause you to be even more unbalanced, which means even more energy loss for you. And mentally you're going to be mad because you missed and gave your opponent that advantage over you.

Dig With Your Knuckles

What this means, is that when you make contact with your opponent you dig your knuckles into whatever area you're hitting. It's just a simple flick of the wrist with your knuckles grinding into your opponent. Actually try to dig or scrape whatever part of the body you're targeting.

This will increase the power of your punch a lot. It also keeps a boxer from hitting with his fingers and absorbing the punch into his fingers. You can feel the solidness of this punch and so can your opponent.

Slip

A slip is basically ducking a punch. To slip a punch, you twist at the hips, bend at the knees, and bend slightly forward always keeping your eyes on your opponent. When practicing this maneuver you must visualize your opponent throwing a punch. Remember to stay on the balls of your feet.

If possible, throw out a jab or a hook to the body the same time you slip your opponents punch. Whenever a punch is thrown there is always an opening to hit on the person throwing the punch. A jab usually means the rib cage under the jabbing arm is open.

An uppercut usually leaves your opponent open for a hook to the head. A right hand is hard to counter because the left side of the head is protected from the left hand and the right shoulder protects the right side to the head. The way to counter a straight right is by an overhand right or an uppercut.

Outside Punches

What I mean by outside punches is punches that you should throw when your opponent is at the end of your punch and not coming in at you and in your chest. Outside punches use the most energy because you're reaching out to your opponent.

Since your opponent is farther away, he will have a greater reaction time to react to your punch. So an outside punch cannot be a lazy punch. It must be quick and delivered with damaging intentions. Outside punches include the jab, hooks, overhand right and straight right.

The Jab

You can frustrate your opponent by continuously sticking him with your jab. Just pepper away at him if you know you're quicker than he is. Every time he throws a punch beat him with a quick jab. It drives a boxer crazy when their opponent constantly has their glove in his face.

The jab is done by holding your hand up high with your elbow in close to your body. Push off your back foot like a pitcher. Step forward with your forward foot and snap your arm straight out at your target. Rotate your fist over (thumb turns inward) as you reach full extension.

Keep your chin to your shoulder to protect your head. You don't need to use a lot of power in this punch. It's used to bait, steer, frustrate, blind, and knock your opponent off balance. It doesn't have to be a powerful punch but it does have to be quick. If done quickly and carefully, the jab is probably your safest punch.

The jab is perfect for baiting your opponent. For example, throw a jab to the body and when your opponent goes to protect his midsection, come up quick with a straight right and a hook to the head.

Or throw a jab to the head. Your opponent will keep his guard up to his head and you can quickly drop down and bang away at his body. You use the jab to steer your opponent by knocking him to one side or the other.

You can also steer him by using your jab as bait. Throw out the jab with intentions of moving quickly to one side or the other. Your opponent will counter your jab and follow you in the direction you are moving.

When you keep your glove in your opponent's face, you blind him. It's hard to see with a glove constantly in face. A boxer's sight is limited already with their own gloves in their face.

By adding your glove to the picture you make it even worse. Using the jab correctly with enough power can unbalance your opponent. An unbalanced fighter is a vulnerable fighter.

Knock your opponent from one side to the other or backward. When you see that your opponent is unbalanced, unleash your combinations and make him pay.

<u>BOXING TRAINING PROGRAM</u>

Note: This program is designed for advanced fighters. If you are a beginner looking for an effective program this one can be modified to suit you. Use the same program at lower intensities. If you have any physical problems (i.e. heart trouble) you will want to consult your physician first.

Before you begin: One rule I follow during training is never slack during training. If you slack during training you will slack during your fight. Always give 100 percent during training and you will give 100 percent during your fight. Boxing is 90 percent mental 10 percent physical. Train your mind to always give 100 percent. Never Give Up!

Summary of program

1. Stretch (5 minutes)
2. Shadow boxing (6 minutes)
3. Arm twirls (3 – 1 min. rounds with one minute break in between)
4. Waist bends (50 revolutions clockwise then counter clockwise)
5. Jump roping (3 – 3 min. rounds with 30 second break in between)
6. Slips (50 left then right)
7. Punching bag (6 – 3 min rounds with 1 minute break in between)
8. Speed bag (4 – 3 min rounds with 1 minute break in between)
9. Crunches (based on individual)
10. Duck walk (based on individual)
11. Pull ups (based on individual)
12. Push ups (based on individual)
13. Jumping jacks (100)
14. Road work (1 – 5 miles based on the individual)

1.STRETCHING

Stretching before a work out is essential in keeping you in the fight. A careless decision of not stretching is a quick way of throwing away weeks of training. A boxer's body needs to be perfectly tuned like a racecar. Every part needs to be in perfect running condition. So always stretch before your workout.

2. SHADOW BOXING

Shadow boxing consists of combining punch combinations, feet work, visualization of opponent, and breathing. I like to use shadow boxing to warm up. Start out with very slow movement and then progress into movement that is quick, under control, and carried out with great concentration. Keep on the balls of your feet. This will give you balance and allow you to absorb a hit better.

3. ARM TWIRLS

Arm twirls consist of holding arms straight out from your sides. Begin by moving arms in a small circular motion. As your arms begin to tire move them in larger circular motions. Then alternate directions.

4. WASTE BENDS

Waist bends consist of four bends in a circular motion. Begin by making one repetition of bending forward, then to the right side, then to the back, then to the left side, and then back to the front. This will help you with slipping jabs, strengthen your abdominal muscles, and build coordination.

5. JUMP ROPING

Jump roping is an important part of a boxing workout. It increases stamina, improves coordination, and strengthens leg muscles. Start off jump roping in one spot. As you loosen up a little more, begin to move forward and then backwards. Then as you progress, began to move side to side, and then move in a circular pattern. For beginning boxers you may want to stay in one spot as your skills improve with jump roping you can progress into the more advanced techniques. While jump roping, raise knees as high as they will go and then let them rest by keeping them at a lower height. Alternate techniques throughout your jump roping session. More in-depth look at Training

6. SLIPS

Practicing slips is just as much mental as it is physical. A slip is basically ducking a punch. To slip a punch, you twist at the hips, bend at the knees, and bend slightly forward always keeping your eyes on your opponent. When practicing this maneuver you must visualize your opponent throwing a punch. Remember to stay on the balls of your feet.

7. PUNCHING BAG

I consider using the punching bag the most fun part of my workout. This is where you can really visualize your opponent in what you want to do to him or her. There are many important things to remember when using a punching bag. To the beginner, combining all aspects will be a great challenge. I suggest taking one aspect at a time and mastering it. First, when throwing a punch, keep muscles loose and snap your punches out. Don't tighten your muscles. This will tire you out and you'll lose your speed. Next, keep your power at the end of your punches. This means that when your fist strikes the bag your arms are fully extended. By doing this, you have more leverage on your punches and thus more power. Hit the bag with your top knuckles and not your finger knuckles. This will give you a solid punch and reduce chances of injury. A lot of boxers make the mistake of slapping their punches. This means they hit with the knuckles of their fingers. When they do this, their punches are not solid ones, their fingers act as shock absorbers. If you know what handed your opponent is, being left or right handed, you need to circle your bag in the direction away from their power hand. For example, if your opponent is right handed, circle to his left. This will keep you out of his power range and keep you from getting knocked out. Keep on the balls up your feet. Never rest on your heels, because if you receive a solid blow you will be knocked backwards or even down. Keeping on the balls of your feet will help you maintain your balance. Always mix up your combination of punches. When a boxer throws the same combination each time, his or her opponent can figure them out and remedy a counter combination. Mix things up! Confuse your opponent by not being predictable. And remember, always keep your hands up.

8. SPEED BAG

Learning to use a speed bag takes a lot of patience. Using a speed bag will increase punching speed, hand-eye coordination, and timing. This is another part of my workout that I enjoy doing the most. Start by hitting the speed bag with one hand. Let the bag make one complete repetition and then hit it on the way back. Meaning, when you hit the bag, let it hit the far side of the platform, and then the front side of the platform, and then as it is halfway back towards the far side of the platform strike it again. This will give you the rhythm you're looking for. It took me a week or two to get used to using a speed bag.

9. CRUNCHES

Doing crunches will strengthen and harden your abdominal area. This will help when your opponent strikes you in that area.

10. DUCK WALK

To do a duck walk you must get in a crouched position keeping your bottom as close to the ground as possible. Hold your hands up high and walk first in a straight line and then backwards. Then walk in a circle clockwise, and then counter clockwise. This will strengthen your legs and give you stamina.

11. PULL UPS

Do your pull ups first with palms facing you and then away from you.

12. PUSH-UPS

When doing push-ups, I suggest doing them on your fingertips. This will strengthen your hands and reduce injury to your hands. I suggest never doing push-ups on your knuckles because enough stress is given to the area when you are punching. For the beginner, I suggest doing your pushups with your knees on the ground. Some call these girl push-ups, but I use them to progress into the harder push-ups where you keep your body straight. Working out is not about being macho, it is about getting in shape in a safe and effective manner.

13. JUMPING JACKS

Jumping jacks are great for your cardiovascular system.

14. JOGGING

Jogging should be done at your individual pace. Always use proper stretching before your roadwork. Boxers do not jog the way regular people do. When we mean roadwork, it is just that - work. When jogging, throw punches, run backwards, shuffle side to side, and if you feel you need to strengthen, carry weights (ankle and wrist weights are ideal). End your roadwork with a cool down walk of a quarter mile. Always dress for the season. If you catch a cold during training you may have just lost your fight.

GOOD LUCK AND HAPPY TRAINING!

Printed in Poland
by Amazon Fulfillment
Poland Sp. z o.o., Wrocław

91154334R00031